Taylor Swift

FOR ALTO SAX

ISBN 978-1-70519-268-9

Hal • Leonard®

Visit Hal Leonard Online at
www.halleonard.com

World headquarters, contact:
Hal Leonard
7777 West Bluemound Road
Milwaukee, WI 53213
Email: info@halleonard.com

In Europe, contact:
Hal Leonard Europe Limited
1 Red Place
London, W1K 6PL
Email: info@halleonardeurope.com

In Australia, contact:
Hal Leonard Australia Pty. Ltd.
4 Lentara Court
Cheltenham, Victoria, 3192 Australia
Email: info@halleonard.com.au

ALL TOO WELL

ALTO SAX

Words and Music by TAYLOR SWIFT
and LIZ ROSE

ANTI-HERO

ALTO SAX

Words and Music by TAYLOR SWIFT
and JACK ANTONOFF

CHANGE

ALTO SAX

Words and Music by
TAYLOR SWIFT

BACK TO DECEMBER

ALTO SAX

Words and Music
TAYLOR SWI

D.S. al Coda

CODA

1., 2.

3.

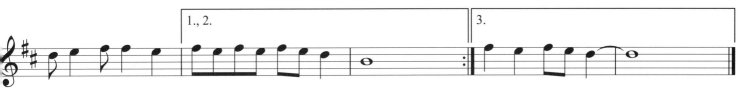

BLANK SPACE

ALTO SAX

Words and Music by TAYLOR SWIFT,
MAX MARTIN and SHELLBACK

To Coda ⊕
D.C. al Coda
(take all repeats)

CODA

CARDIGAN

ALTO SAX

Words and Music by TAYLOR SWIFT
and AARON DESSNER

CHAMPAGNE PROBLEMS

ALTO SAX

Words and Music by TAYLOR SWI[FT]
and WILLIAM BOWE[RY]

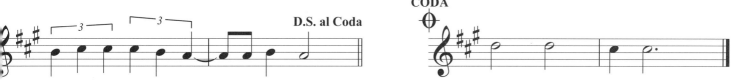

EVERMORE

ALTO SAX

Words and Music by TAYLOR SWIFT,
WILLIAM BOWERY and JUSTIN VERNON

Moderately

To Coda

1.

2.

Faster

accel.

EXILE

ALTO SAX

Words and Music by TAYLOR SWIFT,
WILLIAM BOWERY and JUSTIN VERNON

FEARLESS

ALTO SAX

Words and Music by TAYLOR SWIFT,
LIZ ROSE and HILLARY LINDSEY

FIFTEEN

ALTO SAX

Words and Music by
TAYLOR SWIFT

CODA

D.S. al Coda

I KNEW YOU WERE TROUBLE

ALTO SAX

Words and Music by TAYLOR SWIFT,
SHELLBACK and MAX MARTIN

LAVENDER HAZE

Alto Sax

Words and Music by TAYLOR SWIFT,
ZOË KRAVITZ, JACK ANTONOFF,
MARK ANTHONY SPEARS,
SAM DEW and JAHAAN AKIL SWEET

LOVE STORY

ALTO SAX

Words and Music by
TAYLOR SWIF

MEAN

ALTO SAX

Words and Music by
TAYLOR SWIFT

MINE

ALTO SAX

Words and Music by
TAYLOR SWIFT

THE 1

ALTO SAX

Words and Music by TAYLOR SWIFT
and AARON DESSNER

D.S. al Coda
(with repeat)

CODA

OUR SONG

ALTO SAX

Words and Music by
TAYLOR SWIFT

rit.

PICTURE TO BURN

ALTO SAX

Words and Music by TAYLOR SWIFT
and LIZ ROSE

SHAKE IT OFF

ALTO SAX

Words and Music by TAYLOR SWIFT
MAX MARTIN and SHELLBACK

CODA

SHOULD'VE SAID NO

ALTO SAX

Words and Music by
TAYLOR SWIFT

SPARKS FLY

ALTO SAX

Words and Music by
TAYLOR SWIFT

D.S. al Coda

CODA

SPEAK NOW

ALTO SAX

Words and Music by
TAYLOR SWIFT

SWEET NOTHING

ALTO SAX

Words and Music by TAYLOR SWIFT
and WILLAM BOWERY

D.S. al Coda

CODA

TEARDROPS ON MY GUITAR

ALTO SAX

Words and Music by TAYLOR SWIFT
and LIZ ROSE

rit.

TODAY WAS A FAIRYTALE

ALTO SAX

Words and Music by
TAYLOR SWIFT

51

22

ALTO SAX

Words and Music by TAYLOR SWIFT,
SHELLBACK and MAX MARTIN

53

WE ARE NEVER EVER GETTING BACK TOGETHER

ALTO SAX

Words and Music by TAYLOR SWIFT,
MAX MARTIN and SHELLBACK

WHITE HORSE

ALTO SAX

Words and Music by TAYLOR SWIFT
and LIZ ROSE

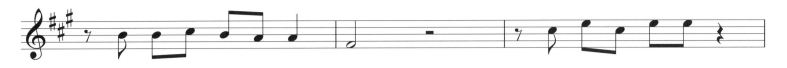

rit.

WILLOW

ALTO SAX

Words and Music by TAYLOR SWIFT
and AARON DESSNER

D.C. al Coda
(no repeat)

CODA

YOU BELONG WITH ME

ALTO SAX

Words and Music by TAYLOR SWIFT
and LIZ ROSE

D.S. al Coda

CODA

YOU NEED TO CALM DOWN

ALTO SAX

Words and Music by TAYLOR SWIFT
and JOEL LITTLE

(small notes optional)

LOOK WHAT YOU MADE ME DO

Alto Sax

Words and Music by TAYLOR SWIFT,
JACK ANTONOFF, RICHARD FAIRBRASS,
FRED FAIRBRASS and ROB MANZOLI